All Scripture references taken from the KJV of the Holy Bible, unless otherwise indicated.

<u>**STEAL, KILL, DESTROY?** ***Why You Came Into Their Life & Why They Came Into Yours***</u>

by Dr. Marlene Miles

Freshwater Press 2026

Freshwaterpress9@gmail.com

ISBN: 978-1-971933-50-4

Paperback Version

Table of Contents

STEAL, KILL, DESTROY

Why You Came Into Their Life & Why They Came Into Yours

RAY & CLAUDIA

Ray came in to Claudia's life... or Claudia came into Ray's life. No one is really sure of how, when, or where it started. We just know that by the time Claudia came to Ray's place, she was really impressed.

Ray’s penthouse sprawled across the top floor, drenched in sunlight from floor-to-ceiling windows that framed a sweeping cityscape. The space was appointed with sleek, modern furnishings—leather sofas, glass coffee tables, and bold abstract art—each piece chosen to reflect his taste for both luxury and comfort. A grand piano anchored the living area--, oh, he played? Oh, yes, he played.

The state-of-the-art kitchen gleamed nearby, ready for spontaneous dinner parties or quiet nights in. Every detail signaled sophistication: the bar cart stocked with rare spirits stood proudly next to the illuminated wine wall, and a private terrace boasting an infinity pool, where Ray would unwind above the city lights.

Ray's home spoke to his status and his zest for living: designer rugs underfoot, curated bookshelves lining the walls, and artful touches that made the space both inviting and impressive. He was single, successful, and thriving, hosting friends on weekends and savoring the quiet moments when he had the place to himself. The penthouse was not only a statement of wealth—it was a playground and a sanctuary, perfectly tailored to a man who enjoyed every bit of what life had to offer.

Before that we know that when Ray first saw Claudia, she was dressed to the nine's wearing and carrying everything designer.

Claudia swept into Ray's penthouse in a tailored Balmain blazer with gold hardware, a silk blouse layered beneath, and sharply pressed high-waisted trousers that elongated her silhouette. Her feet were adorned with red-soled Christian Louboutin heels, and in the crook of her arm rested a quilted Chanel handbag, its chain glinting under the city lights. A Rolex watch flashed at her wrist, and she wore oversized Celine sunglasses, framing her face with effortless glamour. For accents, she carried her phone in a custom Louis Vuitton case and sported a pair of diamond stud earrings, subtle yet undeniably luxe. Every piece she wore was a statement, a blend of power and impeccable taste befitting a woman who knew her worth and dressed to inspire.

He was really impressed. She was out to catch. Ray came into Claudia's life… or maybe Claudia came into Ray's. No one could say exactly when it started, but we do know there was an instant urge to merge.

There wasn't a moment anyone could point to and say, *there—right there—that's when it began.* By the time anyone noticed, they were already in each other's orbit.

What is certain is this: When Ray first saw Claudia, she was unforgettable. Dressed in designer from head to toe, every detail intentional and meticulous. Every movement measured—she did not enter a room quietly. She arrived.

And Ray noticed.

He wasn't looking for anything in particular. At least, that's what he would have said at the time. But he noticed.

Claudia? Claudia did not miss much. By the time she stepped into Ray's space—his world, his environment, his structure—she was already impressed. Everything was in place. Order. Stability. Substance.

It was the kind of place that suggested something had been built… carefully. Deliberately. Protected.

So, it was mutual; Ray liked what he saw and Claudia liked what she saw. She had come… to catch.

She led with her feminine wiles. He led with his bank account, his designer clothes and watches, and his car. He proudly showed his financial wherewithal and success, because he too, was out to "catch."

Claudia knew how to enter a space. Not haphazardly, but with precision. There was a way she carried herself—soft, but deliberate. A glance that lingered just long enough. A smile that suggested interest, but not availability. She did not give everything at once. She understood the power of measure; and she used it well.

Ray responded in kind. Not with words. Not at first. But with presence. The car was not accidental. The watch was not overlooked. The way he paid, the places he chose, the ease with which he moved through certain environments—it all spoke before he did. He did not present himself as a man in need; he presented himself as a man established.

Of course, she noticed. Why wouldn't she? Just as she knew how to draw attention, Ray also knew how to hold it.

What neither of them said—but both of them understood—was this: Something was being offered, and something was being measured. On top of that: something… was being evaluated.

Claudia led with her best assets. Ray led with his resources—his success, his stability, his ability to provide access to a certain kind of life. Each revealed what they believed would attract.

Each watched to see what it would produce. Somewhere beneath the admiration, beneath the conversation… beneath the ease of it all, smarter questions began to form. It was not yet spoken or acknowledged, but it was present.

He didn't wonder if she was the one trying to catch and she didn't wonder if he was because each was so into their own game that they actually thought too much of themselves and not as much as they should have of the other.

From our vantage point, though, we can ask, what were either of them trying to lay hold to and for what reason?

ACCESS & INTIMACY

Access did not announce itself; it never does. It comes quietly—through conversation, through time, through the gradual lowering of boundaries that no longer feel necessary.

What was once observed from a distance… is now suddenly within reach.

By month two, Claudia no longer visited Ray's penthouse as a guest. She moved with a kind of ease that suggested belonging.

Ray? He no longer measured his words as carefully. He no longer watched as closely. There was comfort now. The kind that settles in when something becomes familiar… or when it feels safe enough to stop questioning.

That was the first shift. It was neither loud nor obvious. But it was real. Access, once established, does not remain neutral. It begins to shape, and to influence. It affects small things, at first, like preferences and timing. Decisions made a little differently than before. Nothing alarming. Nothing that could be pointed to and called a problem, but something had changed.

If either of them noticed… neither of them said anything.

This part? This part was not new; Claudia had done this before. This is how this part works. She didn't need to say anything, else she'd look too eager, too needy, too pushy.

Ray had done this before—many times. Maybe too many times. Different faces. Different settings, but the pattern was familiar.

This was how they each worked. This was how they each moved. This was how they caught… what they were out to catch.

Once influence was in place, there was no longer a need to reach. They could relax now. The only need now was to direct.

Chemistry was there, but intimacy did not arrive all at once; that was part of the dance.

Intimacy unfolded, naturally, gradually. Almost as if it had always been on its way.

What began as presence became proximity. What was once observed and desired became experienced. And what had been measured from a distance… was now felt up close.

There was this closeness now that got each of them what they wanted. There was an ease that no longer needed to be earned.

Time stretched differently in each other's company. Conversations softened. Boundaries, once clear, became unnecessary… or so it seemed.

With that closeness came expectation, unspoken, at first, then assumed. Claudia began to expect access—not just to Ray's space, but to what he represented--, stability. Provision. Continuity. Not as a request, but as a given.

Ray, in his own way, began to expect something as well; it was neither stated nor negotiated, but, understood.

He had opened his world. In return--, he expected… return. Attention. Loyalty. Availability. Full access. Permission, as it were. Something that confirmed what he had already begun to invest.

Neither of them paused to define it because neither of them believed it needed to be defined. It felt obvious. It felt mutual. It felt aligned--, but it was not.

Defining it would make them seem uncool and people of their caliber, or their status were never uncool.

In that non-conversation, what each of them expected… did not mirror the other. They did not answer the other. They did not complement each other. Somehow, they were moving closer. They began to become intertwined, tied to the same thread, but on opposite ends of it. The tugging had not yet begun. But, it would.

Growing more connected. Becoming more entangled, and yet, quietly, completely, and without either of them realizing it— they were moving in opposite directions, with very opposite expectations that were not yet visible, not yet disruptive, but already established.

BY THE BOOK

She knows what comes next; she'd done this before and this one is by the book. The book her auntie and her friends taught her. It's unwritten and untitled, but it is: *How to Catch a Man. She's ready for next; she's sure of it.*

He's got his book too--, well, at least the Cliff Notes. To him, what comes next is... nothing. His mission is completed.

Something different than the usual next happened. She expected that *next* was him falling completely and entirely for her. Next was her deciding, taking her time to decide is she wanted to marry him and then dismissing him because he was not good enough. Claudia was so excited because she was not going to dismiss this one. Ray was **the one.**

She had seen it before, felt it before. She had moved through it enough times to know exactly where they were. This was the point where things settled. Where the effort eased… not because interest had faded, but because it had been secured. There was a rhythm to this tango, a sequence, a pattern.

It was not written but learned. It had been passed down in quiet conversations, in knowing glances, in the kind of advice that did not need to be explained in full. Her auntie had called it wisdom. Her friends had called it strategy. Claudia simply knew it as… how it worked.

How to Catch a Man.

According to everything she had been taught—this was the part where it became real. This is when what had been built began to stabilize. It's where presence turned into position and where what was gained… was kept.

She did not question it. Why would she? It had worked before. It had worked more than once; even several times. Or at least… it had appeared to.

Ray felt the shift too, but not in the same way. To him, there was no next phase, no unfolding stage. There was no deeper transition waiting to be navigated. What had been pursued… had been obtained. What had been opened… had been entered. What had been desired… had been experienced.

To Ray, was completion. Mission accomplished, plus she was getting kinda needy lately and that was a turn-off. Ray did not see a beginning; he saw an end. He didn't feel that this end was malicious or unkind; it was just time.

Simply… finally.

He had done what he set out to do. Or at least, what he believed he had set out to do.

Claudia was preparing to build.

Ray was prepared… to rest and recharge. That had been a fun few weeks, or had it been a months, by this time? It was great; she was great, now it's time to move on.

Claudia, on the other hand, was moving into expectation while he was settling into conclusion.

Somewhere between her “now it begins”… and his “it’s already done”… all the unspoken things began to fracture. This breakage wasn’t visible outwardly, just yet, but beneath the surface— where alignment is either confirmed, or quietly undone. There was an invisible tectonic shift.

None of what was in Claudia’s book was in Ray’s playbook. Claudia couldn’t even believe Ray had a playbook. Aren’t men basically simple folks, according to them?

There was definitely a change of pattern and Claudia recognized the shift; it was meteoric, it was atmospheric, it was a clash of high and low pressure, and it would certainly be a storm.

They each had their own plan, but they were quite different from one another. They were not following the same playbook, even though both believed they were doing it *right.* Neither believed or would ever admit they were following a script.

Programming is not a 'script', *or is it?"*

Neither of them would have admitted, if asked, that they were following anything at all. To each, to either of them, this was not performance; this was instinct. This was choice and preference. This is dating. This is how it's done. Everything felt so natural. It all made sense. It worked; they worked together.

But what feels natural is not always original. What feels like choice is not always independent. What is repeated… often has a source.

Claudia called it experience.

Ray called it understanding.

But neither of them stopped to ask a quieter, more unsettling question: *Where did this come from?* Because if it was learned, then it could be traced. If it could be traced, then it was attained from somewhere--, it was not as personal, original, or as organic as it felt. It was not as unique; it was a script. Neither of them would have called it that, however – well at lest on their own part. Each thought they were in the clear, innocent and pure-hearted.

Calling it a script would have felt too controlled, too deliberate, too… exposed. But what is a script, if not a pattern that has been learned, repeated, and trusted?

What is programming? Is it not a script that no longer feels like one?

And what happens when two people meet, each moving with precision, each responding exactly as expected, and each believing they are acting freely. Yet both are following something already written? The result is not alignment. It is collision. Delayed. Unrecognized, but inevitable.

What is programming… if not a script that no longer feels like one?

IT'S DIFFERENT NOW

The first sign was not dramatic. There was no argument. There were no raised voices. There was no moment either of them could point to and say— *that's when something changed. Nobody cheated; nobody disrespected anyone in public; neither of them were unkind to the other.*

Nothing bad had happened, visibly. They were still speaking. Still seeing each other. They were still moving within the same space they had so carefully built. Yet—something did not settle the same way.

Claudia noticed it first, not as a thought, but as a feeling. A moment that he should have affirmed her and their relationship, but he didn't. At that time she wanted to ask, "What is our relationship?" But she didn't. A response that should have followed didn't come; she didn't want to seem uncool, or be the first one to be uncool.

Maybe the response she waned wasn't absent, it was just lighter than expected. It was less anchored, less certain. She did not name it. Why would she? Nothing was wrong—not really. Everything looked the same.

Ray noticed something too. But not in the same way. There was a subtle pressure now. Not spoken. Not demanded, but present. An expectation he could not fully define… but could feel.

Something had shifted from ease… to requirement. From presence… to implication.

He did not question it. Why would he? Nothing had been said. Everything appeared intact. So, they continued even though whatever this was between them wasn't progressing forward, therefore it had begun it's downward spiral.

Ray's script was winning over Claudia's.

She had begun adjusting in small ways, compensating without realizing it. Interpreting without asking. Each responding to something the other had not clearly expressed— and both assuming it was *understood.*

A moment that should have affirmed her… didn't. The shift did not stop. It adapted. What was first felt… but ignored… did not disappear. It recalibrated.

Claudia leaned in. Not noticeably. Not in a way that could be called effort. But in small, precise ways. More presence. More availability. A little more attentiveness where it seemed to matter. Not out of desperation. Out of alignment— or what she believed was alignment.

If something had not landed the way it should have, then something needed to be reinforced. That was how it worked. That was how it had always worked. Ray adjusted too, but in the opposite direction.

Where something began to feel less clear… he created space. Not distance. Just… less immediacy. Less urgency to respond. Less instinct to match what he could feel but not define. It wasn't rejection; it was regulation. Or at least, that's what it felt like to him.

Something had shifted from natural… to expected. And where expectation entered— he instinctively reduced his pace. Neither of them saw it as a problem. They saw it as response, as adjustment, as movement toward balance. They were not balancing; they were compensating.

Claudia was giving more to restore what felt incomplete. Ray was giving less to relieve what felt undefined. And somewhere between her increase… and his reduction, something began to slip. Not taken or removed but no longer held in the same way.

And because nothing had been named— nothing could be corrected. So, they continued. Each doing what made sense. Each following what felt right. Each moving further into a pattern… that neither of them had chosen consciously, but both were now sustaining.

NO HONOR

Something had been lost—or so Claudia believed. Her complaint was simple: he no longer honored her. Ray, on the other hand, questioned what "honor" meant; in his mind, she had already relinquished it. Yet Claudia did not call it loss, not at first. Instead, she named it a lack. To her it was a shift, a subtle absence of something that had once been present without effort. She searched for words and found these: respect, attention, care, but ultimately, she settled on honor.

Honor became the definition for what she felt was missing. She didn't say it immediately, but she felt it—especially in the way he no longer paused the same way when she spoke, in gestures that had become optional, in actions that once seemed intentional but now felt assumed. It wasn't that these things were gone, but they were no longer offered with the same weight. To her, that meant something had been taken. Something had changed. Something that should have remained… had not.

Ray noticed the change, too; not in her, but in the expectation. It was there now: quiet, but present—a demand without words, a standard he had not agreed to but could feel pressing against him. He turned the word "honor" over in his mind, measured it, considered it, and ultimately dismissed it. Not out of disregard, but out of conclusion. For Ray, honor was not something given by assumption; it was something held in regard, protected, reserved. In his mind, this had already been settled—freely, willingly, without request. So what Claudia felt was missing, Ray believed had already been given, or more precisely, was no longer required.

There it was: not spoken, not confronted, but fully present between them. Claudia was looking for something to be at least maintained, but in her playbook there should have been an increase of his esteem toward her by now. After all, she did bring her A game, and her A game had always worked.

Ray was convinced it had been resolved. She believed something had been lost. He believed something had been relinquished. And neither of them knew—they were no longer speaking the same language. She believed something had been lost. “Wait… did I lose this? If I did how?

Did Ray trick me? Or, did I give it away freely?… did I release it?” she wondered.

PATIENTLY

Claudia did not say anything. Not yet. But she began to interpret. At first, it was gentle. She simply noticed that he was quieter, perhaps more distant. She entertained a question that came and went. *Is he busy? Is something going on?* To show her maturity, she didn't press; this would surely impress him she had strategized with her cousin, Jasmine.

But questions, when left unanswered, do not stay neutral. They gather. They connect. They begin to form something more complete, more certain. And slowly, almost without realizing it, she moved from wondering… to concluding. *He's changed.* Not dramatically. Not in a way that could be easily named. But enough. Enough to feel. Enough to notice. Enough to matter. And once that thought settled—everything began to pass through it.

Every delayed response. Every shortened conversation. Every moment that did not carry the same weight it once did. It all aligned. It all confirmed what she had begun to believe. Not because it was proven—but because it fit.

Ray was doing the same. Just… differently. He did not question her behavior. He adjusted to it. What he felt was not distance… but pressure. Subtle. Unspoken, but consistent. There was an expectation that lingered beneath interactions. It was like a need for something to be given… that he no longer felt compelled to provide in the same way. That is how he made sense of it.

She wants more. Not as a complaint. As a conclusion. Simple. Clean. Resolved. And once that settled—his responses followed. Measured. Less immediate. Less engaged where he felt something was being required rather than offered. To him, it was balance. To her, it was withdrawal.

Neither of them believed they were misreading the situation. Neither of them believed they were contributing to it. Each thought they were responding appropriately. Each thought they understood what was happening. And that was the problem. Because once a conclusion feels right—it no longer needs to be questioned. It only needs to be confirmed. And so they continued. Not just interacting—but interpreting. Not just responding—but reinforcing. Each building a version of reality… that the other had never agreed to. Because once a conclusion feels right, it no longer needs to be questioned.

THE SHIFT

It did not begin with a conversation. There was no announcement. No moment where everything stopped and shifted all at once. It began with a realization.

Claudia noticed it before she allowed herself to name it. She felt it as a change in her body, a pattern interrupted, a knowing that came before confirmation. She did not rush to say it. That was not because she didn't understand—but because she did. Some things, once spoken, cannot be returned to silence. So, she held it, for a moment, for a day. Long enough to sit with what it meant before anyone else could.

Ray was not the first to know. How could he be? He had not been the first to notice anything else. By the time she told him, she had already moved through several thoughts he had not yet begun to consider: possibility, outcome, what comes next. He heard the words, but not the same way she did. To Claudia, it was continuation—a progression, something that fit—however unexpectedly—into what she believed had already begun. To Ray, it was interruption. Not of feeling, but of sequence. Something arriving out of order, out of timing, out of alignment with what he believed had already been completed.

He did not say much at first. Not because he had nothing to say—but because he had not yet decided what it meant. Claudia watched him carefully, waiting for something to settle in him the way it had already settled in her. But it didn't—not the same way. And in that moment—more than any delayed call, any unanswered message, any unspoken expectation—the difference between them became clear.

What she saw as a beginning… he experienced as a complication. What she received as something to carry… he encountered as something to consider. And neither of them said it out loud. But both of them knew—this could not be interpreted away.

A pregnancy test may be proof of life, but it is not proof of life of the relationship. It's not the child's responsibility, born or unborn, to hold the relationship of grown people together.

EVERYTHING CHANGES

What she saw as a beginning, he experienced as a complication. Ray did not respond the way Claudia expected. Not with urgency. Not with resolution. Not with the kind of movement that would have turned what she was carrying into something shared.

He listened, he considered, he delayed. And in that delay, something in Claudia began to unravel—not outwardly, not in a way anyone else could see, but internally, where expectation meets uncertainty and uncertainty begins to spiral. Thoughts that once moved in sequence began to collide.

What she had already accepted now felt unstable. What she had begun to build felt unsupported. And what she believed would be secured suddenly felt exposed. The pressure did not come from him alone; it came from what she had already decided this meant, what it should become, what he should do. And when those things did not align, her internal world bore the weight of it.

The loss came quietly. Too early to be seen, too early to be held, but not too early to be felt. And once it happened, there was no returning to what had been before. Claudia did not grieve first.

She interpreted—not slowly, not carefully, but completely. Something had been taken, something had been disrupted, something that should have been protected was not. And in her mind, there was a source. Ray did not experience it the same way. He had not fully entered what she had already begun to carry.

So, when it was gone, he was left with questions she did not have: uncertainty, doubt, a distance from the event that, to her, was undeniable. And that distance felt like dismissal, felt like denial, felt like something else entirely. By the time they stood in the same space again, they were no longer looking at the same situation. Claudia was standing in loss; Ray was standing in ambiguity.

She was asking: Why did you come into my life? To build or to break? To give or to take? To carry or to destroy? He was asking, though not as clearly: What did this become? What was this supposed to be? What did you expect it to turn into? And beneath both of their questions, unspoken but present, was another—one neither of them had asked at the beginning, one neither of them had been willing to consider:

Why did you come? To steal? To kill? Or to destroy? And if not you, then who? Because something had moved through this. Something had taken shape. Something had left its mark. And now, for the first time, they could no longer avoid the question of motive.

Claudia did not grieve first. She interpreted. Claudia was standing in loss. Ray was standing in ambiguity.

TO STEAL

Ray came to steal. He led with all of his best and success, but he never said, never intimated or ever alluded to intention or permanence. They never had the conversation, none of the governing, defining conversations. They were both just cool, whatever that was at that time. He never had intention. He was not looking for permanence; she was. He came to take what he wanted, what he could with plans to dip out after that. Ray came to steal Claudia's time, youth, beauty, style, affection and whatever else she brought to the table.

Their toxicity killed.

Then Claudia wanted to destroy. It did not happen all at once. It unfolded quietly, predictably, in a sequence neither of them recognized while they were in it. But looking back—the pattern was there. Clear. Unbroken.

Ray came with desire. Not to build. Not to remain. But to obtain. To experience. To take what was offered… and what was not fully guarded. He did not call it theft. He would not have recognized it that way. But what he came for—once received—he did not intend to sustain. And that is how stealing works. It does not always look like removal. Sometimes it looks like taking what was never meant to be handled lightly… and leaving nothing in its place.

What formed between them—what they fed, what they ignored, what they assumed—began to weaken what might have otherwise stood. Not by force. By mixture. By misalignment. By two people moving with different intentions… under the appearance of agreement. And that is how things are killed. Not always by attack. Sometimes by what is allowed to develop unchecked.

And when it was gone—when what had been carried was no longer there—something in Claudia turned. Not outwardly at first. But inwardly. Decisively. Because loss, when not understood, seeks a target. And pain, when not resolved, seeks an outlet. What she could not restore—she now wanted to answer. What she could not recover—she now wanted to confront. Not to rebuild. But to make right what she believed had been done. And that is how destruction begins. Not from nothing. But from what has already been wounded.

Steal. Kill. Destroy. Not separate acts. A progression. A pattern. A sequence that, once set in motion—completes itself. Unless it is recognized. Unless it is stopped. Unless someone, at some point, asks the question that was never asked at the beginning: What did I come into this carrying? And what have I now released into it? Steal. Kill. Destroy. Not separate acts. A progression.

TO KILL

This is not their story alone. Patterns do not belong to people—they move through them. Where do you stand in it?

It did not end cleanly. Things rarely do. The conversation that should have clarified... escalated. Not all at once, but quickly enough that neither of them stopped it. Words sharpened. Assumptions surfaced. What had been held beneath the surface now pressed forward—unfiltered, unmeasured.

And then—a moment. A movement. Too fast to reconsider. Too late to undo. Ray pushed her. Not with force meant to injure, but with enough to cross a line that, once crossed, does not return to where it was. Silence followed. Not peace. Not resolution. Just... the absence of what had been before.

Claudia did not respond immediately. She didn't need to. Something had already settled in her—not in her emotions, but deeper than that, in her conclusion. This was no longer confusion. No longer misalignment. No longer something to be worked through. This was now... defined. And once something is defined—it can be acted upon.

She did not call it revenge. That would have required acknowledgment. She called it something else: clarity, accountability, protection, a need to set things in order—to ensure that what had happened did not go unanswered. And so she moved. Not loudly. Not dramatically. But deliberately. What she shared, who she spoke to, what she allowed to be known, what she chose not to withhold anymore—each decision felt justified, measured, even necessary.

Because in her mind—she was not trying to destroy him. She doesn't steal. She doesn't kill. She doesn't destroy—no, not Claudia. She was responding to what had been done. She was correcting what had been left unresolved. She was making sure it would not happen again. But intention does not always define outcome. And what begins as justification can move, quietly and steadily, into something else. Something that does not rebuild. Something that does not restore. Something that does not stop—once it has found direction. And by the time it is recognized—it is already in motion.

"All the ways of a man are clean in his own eyes."

Claudia does not say: "I'm going to destroy him." She says (internally, subtly): "I need closure." "He needs to take responsibility." "People should know who he really is." "I'm just protecting myself." But underneath... the trajectory is destructive.

She did not call it revenge... She called it something else.

I've done this… in my own way.

TO DESTROY

Claudia has no idea that she is "destroying" him. She doesn't possess that level of self-awareness, but someone finally asks her about midbook or beyond: "Why did you come into his life? Was it to steal, kill, or destroy?" Shocked, Claudia exclaims, “WHAT

"Why am I in this person's life? Why are they in mine?" The lesson emerges: from the very beginning, not after disaster, we must ask ourselves if we leave a person better than when we met them, or worse.

It wasn’t said in anger, nor in accusation, not even as correction. That’s what made it land the way it did. They had been talking—about everything and nothing—when the question came. Simple. Unadorned. Almost casual: “Why did you come into his life?”

Claudia didn't answer immediately. The question didn't fit; it didn't match the situation as she understood it. So, she deflected: "What do you mean?" The response was just as steady, "Was it to build?" She frowned, "That's not what happened." A pause. Then—"Was it to steal… to kill… or to destroy?" "What?!" she said, almost laughing—not because it was funny, but because it felt absurd, even offensive. "I didn't come to do anything like that." And she meant it. Completely. Because in her mind—she hadn't. She had come to connect. To grow something. To become something. To secure something. To move forward. That's how she saw it. That's how she would have told it. But the question did not leave. It settled, uncomfortably. Not because she agreed with it—but because she couldn't immediately dismiss it.

And for the first time—not in emotion, not in reaction, but in stillness—another thought, quieter and far less certain, began to form. Not what did he do… but—what did I bring? You're no longer just telling what happened; you're asking yourself: Why are you in this person's life?

From the beginning: discernment, not damage control.

Don't wait until something is broken. Most people do not ask the question at the beginning. They ask it at the end—after something has shifted, after something has been lost, after something has been named. But by then, the pattern has already run its course. The better question is not: "What happened?" The better question is: "What did I come into this carrying?" Because no one enters empty. Not truly. Everyone arrives with something: expectations, needs, intentions—spoken or not, patterns—recognized or not. And what you carry does not stay contained. It moves. It expresses. It shapes. So the question must be asked early—before connection deepens, "Why am I here?" And just as important—"Why are they?"

If you do not leave a person <u>better</u> than when you met them, then why are you or why were you in their lives?

"WHAT!" exclaims Claudia, playing back all the parts of her relationship with Ray in her head. We were just dating. This is how you date. I was following the book; I didn't do anything wrong.

"What?!" Claudia said again—but this time, not out loud. Inside. Sharp. Immediate. Defensive. Her mind moved quickly—faster than the question that had been asked. She began to replay it. Not the end. The beginning. The middle. Every moment that had led here. We were just dating. That's what it was. That's what people do. You meet. You connect. You spend time. You grow closer. You see where it goes. That's how it works. That's how it's done. I didn't do anything wrong.

The thought settled in her—firm, familiar, reinforced. I followed what I was taught. What I saw. What I knew. There was a way this was supposed to go. A rhythm to it. A progression. And she had followed it. Step by step. Just like she had learned. Just like she had seen. Just like she had done before. So how could the outcome be wrong if the process was right? The question pressed again—not from outside this time, but from somewhere she had not been listening to before. If the process was right… why did it end like this? And if it ended like this… was it ever as right as it felt?

“What?!” Claudia repeated, a third time—but this time, the sound of it didn’t settle the way it usually did. It didn’t dismiss the question. It echoed. She leaned back, her mind already moving—retracing, reorganizing, defending. We were just dating. That’s all it was. That’s how it works. You meet someone. You spend time. You get closer. You see where it goes she reiterated for a second or another time. That’s what people do. That’s what everyone does. She followed it back further—the way she presented herself, the way she responded, the way she knew when to lean in and when to hold back. None of it was random. It was learned. Refined. Proven. I followed the process. I didn’t do anything wrong. That thought came quickly. Firm. Rehearsed. Comforting. But this time—it didn’t hold the same weight.

Because something in her could not ignore what had already happened. If nothing was wrong… why did it end like this? If everything was done the way it was supposed to be done… why did it not produce what it was supposed to produce? She didn’t have an answer. Not one she was ready to accept. So instead, she reached for what she had always relied on—

the method. The way. The pattern. The "book." But for the first time—she wasn't asking how to follow it. She was asking something else. Who wrote it? And why did it lead here?

THE *BOOK* YOU DIDN'T KNOW YOU WERE FOLLOWING

Claudia was not confused because she lacked experience. She was confused because she had followed something… correctly. Step by step. Moment by moment. She had not guessed. She had not wandered. She had executed.

Still, the outcome did not match what the process promised.

This raised a question she had never asked before: What if the problem was not how she followed it? What she was following?

Most people do not think of their behavior as learned. They think of it as natural, as instinct. Preference. Personality. But what feels natural is often practiced.

What feels like preference is often patterned. What feels like "this is just how I am"— is often something that was taught, observed, repeated, and reinforced. Long before it was ever questioned.

Claudia called it experience. Ray called it understanding. But neither of them had stopped to ask: Where did this come from? Because if it was learned— then it can be examined.

And if it can be examined— then it is not beyond correction. The problem is not that people follow a pattern. The problem is that they follow it without knowing its outcome, without testing its fruit, without asking what it actually produces— not at the beginning, but at the end.

You can follow a way perfectly… and still arrive at the wrong place. Not because you failed— but because the way itself leads there. And if you never question the way— you will repeat the result

WHAT YOU WERE TAUGHT WITHOUT KNOWING IT

Not everything you follow--, not everything in your 'book' was taught directly, or properly. Some things were absorbed. Some were picked up from observation. Many things were imitated. Some were normalized.

You saw what worked. You saw what gained attention. You saw what secured interest. You saw what kept someone engaged— or appeared to. Then, over time, without realizing it, you formed a way. A method. A pattern that felt like your own— but was built from what you had seen.

The question is not whether you learned something. The question is: What did you learn? And more importantly—

what does it produce?

Sometimes, what you internalized was subtle—so woven into daily routine that you never recognized it as learned. It might have been the silence after disappointment, the way you responded to praise, or how you navigated conflict. These invisible lessons shaped your instincts and reactions before you ever gave them conscious thought. What you did not question, you simply carried forward.

Over time, these patterns became the script you lived by. They guided choices, influenced relationships, and determined how you interpreted the world around you. Yet, unless you pause and examine them, it is easy to mistake these scripts for your true self. The line between learned behavior and authentic identity can be thin—but it is worth investigating.

So, the invitation is to look closer. Consider not only what you learned, but who you learned it from, and why. Ask yourself if these patterns serve you well, or if they simply repeat old cycles. The act of questioning is not just about uncovering roots, but about opening the possibility for change—so that the 'book' you are following truly becomes your own.

RAY WASN'T EXPECTING THIS

Ray didn't bring it up. He hadn't planned to. In his mind, there wasn't much to explain. Things hadn't worked out. That was all. That was enough.

But the conversation found him anyway. They were sitting across from each other—nothing formal, nothing structured. Just time and the kind of quiet that makes room for things that usually go unspoken.

His friend didn't start with questions. He started with observation. "You don't stay," he said.

Ray looked up. "What do you mean?"

A pause. Then, simply, "You don't stay." It wasn't said with judgment, not sharply, but clearly.

Ray leaned back slightly. "That's not—." He stopped. Because even as he started to respond— something in him hesitated.

His friend continued. "You meet young women--, beautiful, successful, confident young women. You connect; you move things forward, and then at some point— you're done. What was the point in meeting them? To become someone temporary in their lives?"

Ray exhaled. "That's not how I see it."

"I know," his friend said. "That's why I'm saying it." Silence settled between them. Not tense. Not confrontational. But present. "You ever ask what you came into their lives for? I mean, Claudia for example, why did you come into her life?" his friend asked.

Ray frowned slightly. "What do you mean?"

"I mean before anything started— before you got involved— what did you want?"

Ray didn't answer immediately. The question felt… unnecessary. He had wanted connection. To 'get' the girl. That was obvious, wasn't it?

The longer he sat with it— the less clear it felt.

His friend didn't rush him. Just waited and then said, "You move like you're finishing something." "Not building it."

Ray looked at him. "What does that mean?"

"It means you engage like there's a point you're trying to reach. And once you get there— you're done."

Ray shifted. "That's not intentional."

"I didn't say it was."

Another pause. Then— "But it's consistent." That landed differently. Not as accusation, but as a pattern.

Ray's mind moved. Not forward. Back. Moments. Conversations. The beginning. The middle. The shift. He had to admit; he had seen it. He just hadn't called it anything. "I didn't take anything from her--, well, nothing more than she was willing to give," he said, more quietly now.

His friend nodded. "Didn't you?"

But, I didn't—

"I'm not saying you meant to." Then—"What did you leave? How did you leave her?"

Pause.

"Ray, how have you left any of the women that you have left?"

Ray had no answer.

His friend continued, "What did you offer her that made her offer you anything--, anything at all?" Ray still didn't answer. So can I guess that whatever you offered her wasn't a really offer at all, but bait, that you promptly took back, like this was a fishing expedition rather than real life?"

Ray didn't answer. Not because he didn't hear the questions, but because he didn't have an immediate response. And that, more than anything else, stayed with him. Because for the first time, he wasn't being asked what happened. He was being asked, *"What did you create?"*

Ray didn't respond right away. Not after he left. Not even when the conversation replayed itself in his mind—clearer now than it had been in the moment. "You don't stay." The words were simple--, too simple to dismiss.

Ray moved through the rest of his day the way he always did. Tasks. Calls. Movement. But something in him was not moving the same way. It was… slower. More aware. Not of everything, just of that.

He had never thought of himself that way. As someone who didn't stay. That wasn't how he saw it. He wasn't careless. He wasn't reckless. He was a professional businessman, as a matter of fact. He didn't go into things trying to leave. If anything— he told himself, he was just moving forward. Seeing what was there. Letting things unfold. That's how it worked. That's how it always worked. But now— that explanation didn't sit the same way. Because when he looked back, not defensively, but honestly— there was a point. Not obvious. Not announced. But consistent. A moment where something shifted. Where what had been engaging… became complete. Not because something ended. But because, to him, it had reached its purpose. And after that—everything felt different.

It didn't feel wrong, just… done. He had never questioned that. Why would he? Didn't he have every right to just stop if he wanted to? It felt natural, and in his pattern, it was expected. He prided himself in knowing when to bow out. It felt normal.

But now—the question wasn't whether it felt normal, the question was: *What did that produce?*

He thought about Claudia. He didn't think about their argument, or about the end of their relationship. He thought about the beginning, and the middle. He thought about what had been built, what had been said and even what had been implied— without being spoken.

He hadn't promised anything. Not directly. So none of this could be his fault. But he hadn't corrected anything either. He was seven years older than Claudia, maybe he should have been more of a man, more of a leader than he was.

No, he continued trying to soothe his own nerves: he hadn't promised her anything, not in the beginning or in the middle of their fling. And that sat with him differently.

Still, for the first time— he wasn't measuring what he had done, he was considering what he had allowed. He was evaluating what had been assumed in his presence, and what had continued— because he did not address it.

I didn't take anything, he had said to his friend and then again to himself. Maybe that was true. Maybe. But it wasn't complete, because something had still been left— unfinished. Unclear. Unstable. And now, he couldn't ignore the other question.

Not what did I intend. But— what did I *leave*? He didn't have an answer. Not a clean one. Not one he could settle on and move past. That unsettled him more than anything else, because it meant this wasn't about what happened. It was about something in him—

that he had never stopped to examine because his 'system' had always worked.

Until now.

Interrupting his thoughts, his mother called. He answered. "Hello."

"Hello son, how are you?" How's Claudia?

"Mom, Claudia and I broke up."

"Ray! She was a good one why have you dumped *another* girl?"

"Mom how can you say it was me?"

"Because you are my son; I know you. Why do you keep going into those ladies lives and then leaving them hanging?" Ray heard his mother's voice drift off talking to his dad in the background, and some funny noise like she was fumbling with the phone. "Claudia's gone. That good girl; I liked her, but now they are broken up; I don't know what's wrong with your son, Roger. I don't know when we will ever get grandchildren." Then she hung up. She finally hung up.

IT'S NOT JUST THEM

Ray is not the only one who has moved this way. Claudia is not the only one who has felt this way. This is not their pattern alone. It is one that repeats through different people, in different forms, with different outcomes—that, when examined closely, begin to look the same. Because patterns do not belong to individuals, they move through people and cultures and life. Patterns are followed and repeated, silently demanding obedience even to their distortions. They are passed along—until someone stops long enough to see them clearly.

So, the question is no longer: *What did Ray do?* It's not, *What did Claudia feel?* The question is: Where does this pattern show up in you? This is a real question not for theory or assumption, but in reality and in what has already happened. What you have experienced. What you have repeated. What has followed your connections—consistently?

This doesn't just apply to dating or romantic relationships. These same tests and rules need to be used with family, friends, neighbors, and even in business.

What has followed you based on how you interact with and deal with people, opportunities, chances, access, and situations?

Once you can see it there—you can no longer place it entirely outside of yourself. And until you see it, change is not really possible.

THE FRUIT TEST

There is a simple way to test what you are following. Not by how it feels. Not by how it begins. But by what it produces. At the end. Not in the moment of connection—but after the process has run its course. What is left? Clarity—or confusion? Strength—or instability? Peace—or pressure? Do you leave with more understanding—or more questions? Because whatever your way produces—that is what it is designed to do. Not occasionally. Consistently. Patterns are not random. They are reliable. And if you do not examine the result—you will keep trusting the process.

This is the heart of the "fruit test": evaluating the outcome rather than the intention or the comfort of the journey. It is common to judge a path by how it feels in the beginning, the excitement of a new experience, or the reassurance of a familiar routine. But lasting change and growth are measured by the tangible results they leave behind. If what you follow produces chaos, strain, or uncertainty time and again, it is worth asking whether the method itself is flawed—no matter how convincing the initial promise may have been.

To apply the fruit test means to step back and look honestly at the patterns in your life. Are your relationships marked by trust or by repeated disappointment? Does your work leave you with a sense of fulfillment or recurring frustration? Do your daily habits build you up or break you down? These questions are not about assigning blame, they are about recognizing the quiet power of consistency. What you nurture, whether intentionally or by default, will grow. If you want to live differently, you must be willing to evaluate not just what you hope for, but what is actually taking place.

Change begins with awareness. The courage to examine the end of a process, rather than getting lost in excuses for why things "should have" worked, is what separates growth from stagnation. Patterns reveal themselves in outcomes—over days, months, and years. When you hold your way up to the fruit test, you empower yourself to make different choices, to rework your approach, and to align your actions with the results you truly desire. In this way, the fruit test becomes not just a measure, but a catalyst for meaningful transformation.

YOUR LIFE: WHERE THERE MAY BE STEALING, KILLING, OR DESTROYING AND YOU ARE NOT AWARE OF IT..

Patterns do not stay contained to one area. If something is operating in one place—it is often present in others. Not always in the same form. Not always as obvious. But consistent in outcome. So it is worth asking: Where else might this be showing up—without being recognized?

Not only in relationships. But in how you move. How you respond. How you handle what is placed in your care. Because taking does not always look like theft. Sometimes it looks like: withdrawing more than you give. Receiving without sustaining. Leaving others to carry what you helped create.

Killing does not always look like force. Sometimes it looks like withholding what would have brought clarity. Allowing something to weaken through neglect. Participating without intention to maintain.

Destruction—does not always appear dramatic. Sometimes it looks like repeated breakdown, unresolved patterns, or cycles that never complete in a healthy way.

So, look honestly, not defensively, not generally, but specifically. Where have I taken—without considering what I left? Where have I allowed something to weaken—because I did not address it? Where have I participated in outcomes—that consistently end the same way?

What you do not recognize—you cannot correct. And what you do not correct—will continue to produce.

Stealing may be present if: You consistently receive more than you contribute. You benefit from connection without sustaining it. You leave others to resolve what you helped begin.

Killing may be present if: Things weaken in your care. Clarity is avoided. What begins with strength does not remain that way.

Destroying may be present if: The same kind of breakdown follows your involvement. Connections do not end—they collapse. What you are part of does not remain whole.

WHY ARE YOU IN THIS PERSON'S LIFE?

Before connection deepens, it is essential to pause and reflect. Before you grant someone access to your inner world or allow them to influence your decisions, a crucial question should be considered. This inquiry should not be postponed until changes have occurred or feelings have intensified; it must be addressed right at the beginning. The question is simple yet profound: Why am I here?

Instead of focusing on what you feel or what you want, it is important to examine what you bring into a relationship. No one enters any connection empty-handed; everyone carries something with them—whether it be expectation, need, desire, or intention, whether clearly defined or not. What you bring does not remain static; it moves, expresses itself, and ultimately shapes the dynamics between you and the other person.

So, ask yourself clearly: Am I here to build, to take, to secure something for myself, to fill an unaddressed void, or to gain something I believe this person can provide? Equally important is asking why the other person is present in your life. If these questions are not asked at the start, you will be forced to interpret motives and outcomes at the end, which is always more difficult than discerning them from the outset.

If you do not leave a person better than when you met them, you must consider what you have left them as. Were they unchanged, or were they diminished by your presence? Many never reflect on this because they assume their presence is neutral—but it is not. You either contribute to building someone, or you participate in something that does not. What does not build will, in time, break down.

Leaving them better than you found them does not mean losing yourself or shrinking. You do not set yourself on fire to warm them or bow down so they can stand on you. When you leave them better than you find them; you both should be better from that relationship or connection as well.

WHY DO YOU HAVE TO LOWER THEM BEFORE YOU LEAVE?

Why is it so difficult to leave someone as they were? Why does the exit so often require reduction—a lowering, a diminishing, a quiet (or sometimes not so quiet) reframing of who they are? Not always out loud, but internally. Definitively. They become less—less valuable, less worthy, less significant than they once appeared. Why? Why can't the connection end without altering the person? Why must something be taken on the way out?

Some call it closure. Some call it clarity. Some call it seeing things for what they really are. But if that were all it was—why does it so often leave the other person diminished? Why does it not simply release, but instead a reduction or a diminishing?

There is something in us that struggles to walk away while still acknowledging value. Because if we admit there is still something good—something real—something worth keeping—then leaving becomes more difficult, more costly, more honest.

Girl, you left a man that good?

Man, you left *her*? *Her?*

This can't be because we were taught to clean our plates before we left the table, was it?

Not everything you were taught is wrong. But not everything you were taught is right. And some of what you learned was never meant to be applied the way you are applying it now.

"Finish what you start." "Don't waste." "Make it work." "Stay committed." On their own, these sound like wisdom. They make you feel like you're responsible, mature and disciplined. But when they are carried into places they were never meant to go, they stop building. They begin to bind. Because not everything should be finished. Not everything should be made to work. Not everything should be sustained simply because it began.

Some things should be stopped. Some things should be questioned. Some things should be left. Not because you lack discipline—but because you have discernment.

You were taught to finish your plate. But no one told you what to do if what was placed before you was not good for you. So, you stayed in that relationship. You adjusted. You explained it. You tried to make it make sense. Because leaving felt like failure. But staying produced something else.

And that is where the conflict begins. Because what you were taught to value may be the very thing keeping you in what is not right. So now you must examine it. Not emotionally. Not defensively. But clearly.

What have I been following that does not produce what I thought it would? What have I been calling wisdom that is actually repetition? What have I been honoring that I should have questioned?

Once you can see that clearly, once you can answer those questions honestly, you are no longer bound to it. You are no longer required to finish what should have been stopped. And you are no longer obligated to carry what was never meant to remain.

Not all damage comes from bad decisions. Some of it comes from applying the right principles in the wrong place. When that happens, the outcome is not correction. When you believe you are doing the right thing while producing the wrong result, that is deflating and it is confusion. That is harder to confront than doing something you knew was wrong from the start.

So, instead—we adjust the narrative. We lower the value. We redefine the person. Not always because it is true—but because it makes the exit easier to justify. And sometimes, more than justify: to take. Because if there is still something in them that we want—attention, affirmation, validation, resource, presence—then leaving does not always mean releasing. It can mean extracting, wringing out what remains before stepping away. Not always consciously, not always intentionally, but consistently enough to ask the question: Did you leave, or did you take on your way out?

If something in them was still good—still whole—still intact—why was it not left that way? Why did it have to be reduced first? Is it because what we cannot walk away from cleanly, we often change until we can. What we change, we do not always restore. This exposes exit behavior as part of the pattern.

What are you *taking or planning to take on the way out?* "Did I simply leave them… or did I diminish them first?" Did you just leave… or did you take on your way out?

If the people you meet, interact with, and eventually leave all look the same when you go— then what you are following may not be a consequence. It may be a pattern. And patterns that repeat without interruption… begin to look less like accidents— and more like assignment.

So, ask it plainly: Do you leave people better than when you found them— or is it steal, kill, destroy?

Why can't you leave someone until you degrade them, downgrade them or condemn them? Is it because if you think there is any good left in them, you want to wring it out-- for yourself? then NEXT

WHY DID YOU COME?

Did you come to steal, kill, or destroy? It is not always a question that can be answered at the beginning. Because at the beginning, everything feels different. Connection feels genuine. Interest feels mutual. Movement feels natural. Nothing appears harmful. Nothing suggests loss. Nothing signals what it will become. So the question, when asked too early, can feel misplaced, unnecessary, even offensive. Of course not. Why would I come to do that? That is how most would answer. And they would mean it.

But some questions do not reveal their answers in the moment. They reveal them… in the aftermath. After something has shifted. After something has been weakened. After something has been lost. Only then does the pattern begin to take shape. Only then can you trace it. What was taken? What changed? What no longer remains as it once was?

And as you follow the sequence backwards—not emotionally, but honestly—you begin to see what you could not see while you were in it. Not because it was hidden, but because it had not yet completed. Some intentions are not recognized at entry. They are revealed by outcome. Not what you said you came to do. Not what you believed you were doing. But what your presence produced. That is the evidence. That is the answer.

Sometimes—it is only in hindsight that you can say, with clarity: Something was taken. Something was weakened. Something was brought to an end, maybe not all at once, but in sequence. Once seen—it cannot be unseen. Which raises the question, not for the past—but for what comes next. Now that you can see it… what will you do differently?

"Some intentions are not recognized at entry." If the people you meet, interact with and eventually leave all look the same when you go, then your pattern might be an assignment and not simply a consequence. Do you leave them better than when you found them, or is it steal, kill, and destroy?

How long does it take—before something begins to break? Is it immediate? Does it begin the moment disappointment enters? The first unmet expectation. The first shift. The first time something does not land the way it was supposed to. Or was it already in motion long before that moment?

Demolition does not always begin with an event. Sometimes it begins with a structure that was never aligned to begin with. Sometimes it is built on assumption, on expectation that was never stated, or on intention that was never examined. When something is built that way, it does not need to be attacked to fall; it only needs time. So, when the disappointment comes, it feels like the cause, but it may only be the reveal. The moment where what was already unstable can no longer hold.

Some respond to that moment by pulling back. Others respond by pressing harder trying to recover, trying to correct, trying to force alignment where it never existed. When that does not work, something shifts again, from confusion… to conclusion, and then from conclusion… to response.

That response, if left unexamined, can begin to move in a different direction entirely. Not to build. Not to restore. But to answer. To correct. To make right what feels wrong. And somewhere in that movement—without being named, demolition begins. Not always because it was the original intention. But because it became the response.

Yet—in some cases—if you look closely enough—you may find that the foundation itself was never designed to hold anything beyond the beginning.

Which raises a harder question: Was this something that broke… or something that was always going to break?

When what is already in you is triggered, it is not been placed there by someone else; it was always there. What triggers a person is often not the cause; it may be the reveal.

Demolition does not always begin with an event; it begins by choice. It wasn't something that was turned may have been something that was always headed there?

WHAT DID YOU COME CARRYING?

No one enters empty. No one enters with no history. You may arrive without a plan, without a script that you are aware of, but you do not arrive without something. You bring it with you—sometimes quietly, sometimes hidden beneath what feels like genuine connection. But it is there, and it will surface. The question is not whether you carried something into the connection. The question is: What was it?

Did you come looking for validation? To feel seen, chosen, affirmed in a way you had not been before? Did you come for provision—not just financial, but stability, security, access to something you did not yet have on your own? Did you come for identity? To become something through association, to step into a role that gave you weight, position, or meaning?

Did you come to take—not in a way you would name as theft, but in a way that drew from the other person without equal awareness of what you were giving? Did you come to control, to shape the outcome, to guide the direction, to ensure it became what you needed it to be? Or did you come to build, to contribute, to strengthen, to leave something better than you found it?

Whatever you carried in does not stay contained—it moves, it expresses, it takes form, and eventually, it produces. So, before you ask what went wrong, ask what was present from the beginning. What you carried in may be what played out in the end.

> .. and with his tail he took a third part of the stars.. (Revelations 12:4).

There is a pattern that does not always announce itself as destruction. It does not always begin with force. Sometimes it appears as departure, as separation, as movement away. We see in the verse above, even in leaving, something else happens. *"...and with his tail he drew a third part of the stars..."* This is willful; he drew them. They were caught in the motion of something already in decline. There are people who cannot leave alone—not because they are aware of it, but because something in them pulls as they go. Attention, reputation, confidence, clarity. They exit, but they do not release. They withdraw, but not without impact.

What could have remained intact is altered in the process—not always by intention, but by effect. The question must be asked: *When you left, what followed you?* Also ask, *What fell because of it?*

There is a phrase people who like to blame will reach for when something escalates beyond what they expected. "Look what you made me do." It feels accurate in the moment. Because something was triggered. Something shifted. Something moved that had not been active before. The presence of a trigger does not mean the origin was external. What is activated must first exist. It may be unexamined, unaddressed, unrecognized, but it is not newly created. It is revealed.

The other person may have disappointed you. They may have failed to meet expectations. They may have withdrawn, delayed, misaligned, or refused. But they did not place in you the response that followed. They encountered it. They activated it. But they did not create it.

Because if something in you can move toward reduction—toward retaliation—toward tearing down what you once engaged—then that movement was already present. Waiting. Not always consciously. Not always intentionally, but available.

This is where responsibility becomes clear, not for what was done to you, but for how you respond to it. You cannot always control what enters your life, yet you are accountable for what is released from you. If what is released brings harm, then it must be examined, not justified, not explained away, but brought into the light. What is left unexamined will be activated again.

People are often triggered, but what emerges is simply what was already inside them. Not every destructive reaction starts with anger.

Some responses begin with fear, such as the fear of being left, the fear of not being chosen, the fear of rejection.

When that fear becomes powerful, it refuses to stay hidden. It reacts. The question, "You're going to leave me?" may be spoken aloud or remain unspoken, but its presence is unmistakable. It isn't curiosity; it's resistance.

For some, being left isn't just an ending—it's a loss of identity, a loss of control, a loss of something essential they feel compelled to hold onto.

When fear is triggered, the response is rarely release. Instead, it can morph into prevention—control, pressure, or something else entirely. If those attempts fail, another tactic emerges: "If I cannot keep you, I will not let this end cleanly."

This statement is not always spoken, but it is frequently expressed—through escalation, through conflict, through making the exit more painful than it should be. Destruction was not the original intent; it is simply that the loss was intolerable.

What begins as fear, if left unexamined, can transform into something else entirely—not to build or to restore, but to break what can no longer be held.

This is not strength—it is merely reaction. When reaction goes unchecked, it damages rather than preserves.

So, the question is not just, "Do you fear being left?" but "What do you become when that fear is activated?"

"If I cannot keep you—I will not let this end cleanly." "This is not strength. It is reaction." "What do you become when that fear is activated?"

Isn't this the same behavior of the person who ruins a house he is evicted from? Only this time it's not houses or property--, it's people.

DID YOU DRAW THIS TO YOURSELF

It is easier to identify what was done to you… than to consider what may have drawn it. Because what is done to you feels external.. Something you can point to. Something you can name. Something you can separate yourself from.

There is another question that is often avoided, because it is uncomfortable. That question is: Did something in you… *align* with what entered? It agreed--, well, not intentionally or consciously, but in pattern, or in expectation. It matched what you were willing to accept, overlook, or participate in.

What you carry… does not only express outwardly, but it also responds. It recognizes. It connects, and sometimes— it agrees with what it should have resisted. This is not about blame. It is about alignment. You do not draw everything that happens to you, but you do participate in what you remain aligned with.

If something continues, it is worth asking, What in me is allowing this to stay? What is not confronted, is accommodated. What is accommodated— is eventually normalized.

So, ask these questions plainly: *What did I see... but not address? What did I feel... but explain away? What did I allow... because it was easier than confronting it?*

What you agree with, you give permission to remain. What remains— will continue to produce.

Awareness is not condemnation. It is correction. And what is corrected— does not have to be repeated. If the same outcomes continue to appear— then it is no longer enough to explain them.

They must be examined. Not to accuse— but to understand what is being repeated. Because what is repeated without awareness… will continue without interruption.

A string of broken hearts is not a trophy. Likewise, a parking lot of scratched vehicles is nothing to brag about. Acts of revenge, online blasts, calling the person's employer, family member, new love interest or exes, no matter how often repeated—do not represent true strength or power. These repeated actions are not signs of power, they are signs of repetition. They reveal a pattern that remains unbroken and unchallenged.

Real power builds: it governs; it leaves things better than it found those things. Those things are things, and they are people.

Destruction, on the other hand, does not. Destructive actions cycle back, they return again and again, repeating themselves through different people until someone finally recognizes the pattern.

So, the real question isn't how many times it has happened, but whether the cycle will be recognized and interrupted.

The question is: Why does it keep happening through you?

You are of your father the devil, and you want to carry out your father's desires. He was a murderer from the beginning and does not stand in the truth, because there is no truth in him. (John 8:44)

This is not about identity. It is about alignment. It is about what is being expressed… through action. Because anything that moves toward: taking, reducing, ending what should have remained— is not neutral. It follows a pattern. And patterns have a source. The question is not: Who are you?

The question is: What are you agreeing with… when you move this way?

At some point, it is no longer what happened to you— it is what continues to move through you.

THE MOMENT YOU TURN

It does not begin as destruction; it begins as injury. Something did not land the way it should have; something was not given that was expected. Something shifted—subtly at first, then undeniably. And in that moment, there is a choice. Not always recognized. Not always named. But present.

You can remain in what was felt—hurt, disappointment, confusion—and allow it to be processed. Or you can move. Not away from it, but through it, and into something else. The shift is quiet, almost imperceptible. It sounds like: "This isn't right." Then: "This shouldn't have happened." Then: "This needs to be corrected." Somewhere between correction and response, the direction changes. It is no longer about understanding; it becomes about answering. Not to restore, but to make right. To balance. To respond in kind.

That is the moment—not when harm was first felt, but when the decision was made to return it. That decision, that choice was not always conscious or intentional, but because from that point forward, your actions no longer move toward resolution. They move toward impact.

Words sharpen. Silence becomes strategic. Information becomes selective. Presence becomes conditional. What was once connection becomes position. This is the turn. This is not caused by others. No one placed it in you; it is chosen—in response to what was felt. And once that turn is made, the pattern advances: Steal. Kill. Destroy. Not as an identity, but as a direction. Unless it is recognized, and then addressed, it will not stop on its own.

If any of those directives are being followed, if any of those are desired results, then the question should be asked, Who is running this? Who is inspiring or influencing the plan, the response, or the reaction?

We've all been hurt, but we get to choose how we will respond and how we will seek and receive healing.

HOW TO CATCH IT BEFORE IT TURNS AGAIN

You cannot stop what you do not recognize. If a person cannot see that they turn the tables on people and situations there is no way they can manage that and themselves when things arise. If a person goes into fits of rage or anger, pouting or pity fests, to revenge plots when they don't have their way or are disappointed, they are not well-governed.

A turn from what is normal or civil to something more dastardly does not announce itself loudly. It begins in thought, in the mind. It begins in how a person sees things – in interpretation.

Before any action, there is a narrative. A person may feel or say within themselves, "This wasn't right." "They shouldn't have done that." "This needs to be addressed."

Those thoughts are not wrong, but what follows them— determines direction.

The governed person must learn to catch the shift early, not after words that cannot be taken back are spoken. The person needs to remain calm before untoward after actions are taken.

So, at the point of interpretation, ask yourself: What am I about to do with what I just felt? Am I moving toward clarity— or toward reaction? Am I moving toward response or recklessness? Am I seeking understanding, or preparing to answer?

The turn begins here; it also begins in the mind. If you can pause here— you can stop it. Not by suppressing what you feel— but by refusing to let it direct you without examination.

You do not have to follow every thought to its conclusion. You can interrupt it. You can question it. You can refuse to move with it. That is if you have agency and you are self-governed.

In that refusal—the pattern weakens. Because what is not followed…does not establish.

On the off chance that a person is not governed but is influenced by spiritual dynamics that don't mean that person or anyone they deal with any good, the pattern will deepen and possibly become embedded.

HOW TO DISCERN BEFORE YOU ENTER

Discernment is not suspicion. It is not fear, nor is it hesitation rooted in past harm. Discernment is clarity—clarity that comes before involvement deepens and before emotion attaches. Most people wait too long, asking the right questions only after access has been granted, after influence has begun, and after emotional investment has taken hold. However, discernment belongs at the start, before you invest, before you adjust, and before you interpret. It is the ability to see clearly before you become deeply entangled.

When practicing discernment, ask yourself: What is this producing already? Not what it promises, not what it feels like, but what is it actually producing? Is there clarity, or confusion? Is there steadiness, or pressure?

Is there mutual movement, or quiet imbalance? These questions help you understand the true nature of what you're entering into, rather than being swayed by potential or emotion.

Equally important, ask: Who am I becoming in this? Are you becoming more grounded, more whole, more aligned—or are you feeling more uncertain, more reactive, or more dependent on the outcome? Because whatever is present early in the process will not correct itself later; it will only deepen. Discernment is not about preventing connection. Rather, it prevents misalignment from being mistaken for connection. It ensures that clarity guides you before you move forward, protecting you from deepening involvement with something that does not serve you.

HOW TO INTERRUPT THE PATTERN

Patterns do not stop on their own; they tend to run their course and complete themselves unless something intervenes. Left unchecked, these patterns will continue to shape behaviors and outcomes because they are inherently self-perpetuating. To halt their progression, intentional action is required. Otherwise, the cycle simply repeats.

The process of interrupting a pattern does not start with immediate action. Instead, it begins with recognizing the pattern as it unfolds. This means becoming aware of its presence and understanding it as more than just isolated incidents; it is a sequence that follows a certain path. Seeing the pattern clearly is the first step toward making meaningful change.

To truly recognize a pattern, you must observe what initiated it, what allowed it to persist, and what it ultimately produced. Once you have this awareness, you are faced with a decision. This decision should not be made emotionally or in reaction to the moment, but with clarity and intention. You must conclude that the pattern cannot continue—not because of external factors or individuals, but because of the consequences it brings.

Interrupting a pattern can take many forms. Sometimes it looks like creating distance, slowing down, choosing silence, or refusing to respond in familiar ways. It may also require confronting truths that have been avoided. Regardless of the method, the interruption must be deliberate. What is not examined is destined to be repeated, and repetition soon becomes habit.

Breaking a pattern is not accomplished by wishing things were different. The change occurs when you consciously decide to stop participating in the cycle. By refusing to engage with the pattern any longer, you deny it the opportunity to become further established in your life.

Not everything is meant to continue. And not everything that ends is a failure. Some things are meant to be released—not forced, not prolonged, not carried beyond their proper place, but released. Cleanly. Without reduction. Without the need to damage what you are leaving behind.

Healthy release does not require you to rewrite the other person. It does not require you to lower their value so your decision feels justified. It does not require you to take something on your way out to feel like you did not leave empty-handed, or to fulfill an evil prophecy that they won't prosper without you. Instead, it requires something else: clarity.

You recognize what is. You acknowledge what is not. And you respond accordingly—without escalation, without retaliation, without the need to make the ending more than it already is.

Not every ending needs to be answered. Some simply need to be accepted. Once accepted, they are allowed to remain as they are—without interference, without further impact, without additional damage. This is release. Not avoidance. Not denial. But decision.

You do not stay where you should not remain, and you do not destroy what you choose to leave. You exit with awareness, with restraint, and without carrying forward what should have stopped with you. Because what you release cleanly does not continue *through* you, and what does not continue, does not repeat.

This is strength, not in holding on, not in reacting, but in knowing when to let go and doing so without harm.

Did you go in with clean hands? Clean motives? Or were soul ties or massive entanglements created? That will determine how easily or how cleanly you can get out. If you went in with an evil motive it will be hard to leave without bitterness. One reason is you may be resentful that you didn't achieve what you set out to achieve. They are still standing and you did not get what you came for. The other person may not be doing anything at all to you; they've gone on with their life, but that seems to be bothering you.

HOW TO GET RID OF IT PERMANENTLY

Catching the pattern is one thing. Removing it is another. Because what has been repeated becomes familiar and won't leave easily.

It waits. It watches. It looks for another moment to activate—another disappointment, another misalignment, another opportunity to move the same way again.

So, the question is not only: Can you stop it once? The question is: Can you remove it so it no longer directs you? This requires more than awareness. It requires decision.

You must come to a clear conclusion: This is not how I move. This is not how I move when I am hurt, disappointed, or when something does not go the way I expected.

Whatever you leave room for, it will return—not as something new, but as something familiar. That is when the embedding starts. The deeper it gets in, the harder it is to get it out.

You must address it directly, not vaguely, not generally, but specifically. Where have I responded this way before? What have I justified? What have I allowed to continue because it felt deserved?

Once you see it, you do not negotiate with it. You reject it. You refuse agreement with it. You refuse to call it justified. You refuse to call it necessary. What you justify, you permit. What you permit, you repeat. This is where correction becomes permanent—not because the opportunity will not come again, but because when it does, you will not move the same way.

The pattern may present itself, but it will not find agreement. Without agreement, it cannot operate. It cannot direct. It cannot complete its course. Resist, don't agree.

None of us are trying to become someone who is never tested, we are becoming someone who does not continually move in wrong ways when tested.

HOW TO LEAVE WITHOUT DESTROYING

Leaving is not failure. Not always. Not every connection is meant to continue. But how you leave… matters. Just like the relationship or the connection, itself, how things are ended are important. Departure is not neutral. It carries impact.

Some leave quietly—and everything remains intact. Others leave—and something collapses behind them. Not because collapse was intended—but because of what was taken… what was said, and what was altered on the way out.

"…and with his tail he drew a third part of the stars…" There are exits that pull others down. There are exits that release—cleanly without reduction, without degradation, and without the need to redefine the other person in order to justify leaving.

To leave without destroying—you must resist the urge to lower them to make your exit easier. You do not take what remains because it is still available. You do not rewrite the narrative so you do not have to confront your part. You definitely do not run a campaign in public or private to shame, humiliate, or ruin them.

Instead—you leave with clarity. With boundaries. With truth that does not need to injure to be valid. And with restraint. Because not everything you can say… should be said. Not everything you can take… should be taken. And not everything that ended… needs to be broken. You leave decently and in order.

A clean exit does not mean nothing happened. It means what happened does not continue to produce damage after you are gone. Untie, disentangle without violence.

WHAT DID YOU AGREE WITH WITHOUT KNOWING IT?

Not everything that enters your life is forced. Some things are a choice whether you will receive them or not. Some things are verbally accepted and allowed entrance into a life. Some things are allowed in non-verbally, with actions and not so much words. Some things are allowed in by what is tolerated, or what is embraced or celebrated.

With the quiet decision not to address what does not feel right, a person can exclude negative forces from making suggestions or operating in their life.

However, agreement does not always sound like "yes." Sometimes it sounds like silence. Some things you have to verbally say

NO to, or a non-No, or no response at all means yes. Let your No be No.

Sometimes agreement looks like continuation. Sometimes it feels like: procrastination--, "I'll deal with it later."

Whatever you do not confront, you accommodate. What you accommodate— you eventually normalize. So, ask it plainly:

- What did I see… but not address?
- What did I feel… but explain away?
- What did I allow… because it was easier than confronting it?

What you agree with— you give permission to remain.

You don't draw everything that happens to you; no one is that powerful. But a person will sustain what you stay aligned with. The more you repeat the pattern, good or bad, the more embedded it becomes. The more embedded it is, the more you attract more of the same. So the question, Why do I keep meeting these same kinds of people? – needs another question: Are you reacting or responding the same to all these same kinds of people? That could be why it keeps repeating. As long as there is Mercy, it keeps repeating, until you get it right.

QUESTIONS TO ASK BEFORE YOU ENTER AGAIN

By the time most people understand what happened, it has already happened. The pattern has already moved. The outcome has already taken shape. The questions come late: What went wrong? What changed? What should I have seen?

There is a better question—one that belongs at the beginning, not the end. Before connection, before access, before influence, ask it clearly: *Why am I here?*

Don't ask, What do I feel? Don't ask merely, What do I hope? Instead, ask, What do I bring? To make a different, to become different, to connect with different people and situations differently, you will need to be different and bring something different.

You will bring something. You always do, we all do. If we are good, we bring expectation, desire, hope need, intention—formed or unformed. If we are nefarious, we may bring far worse things, but whatever we bring, it will not stay hidden. It will move. It will express. It will produce.

So, ask and answer it honestly: Am I here to build? To contribute? To strengthen what already exists? Or am I here to take? To secure something for myself? To fill something I have not yet addressed? And then—ask the second question. Why are they here? Because discernment is not about suspicion. It is about clarity.

Is there a cost to this?

What is that cost?

Will this be a real blessing, or will it bring sorrow?

Clarity may come after the fact, but you need it before involvement, intertwining, soul tying or entanglement. You cannot control what someone else carries, but you are responsible for what you bring. If you can answer that clearly, you will not have to ask, later, what went wrong. Because you will have seen it… from the start.

REFLECTION

Take a moment to consider what moved through you.

- **Where have I entered without clarity?**
- **What did I expect… without naming it?**
- **What did I take… without recognizing it?**
- **What did I leave behind… that was not whole?**

Going forward—

- **What will I refuse to carry into the next connection?**

Awareness is not condemnation; it is correction. What is corrected— does not have to be repeated.

PRAYER

Father,

Bring clarity where I have assumed understanding.

Reveal what I have carried without examining.

Show me where my ways have felt right… but have produced what is not right.

Give me discernment before I enter, not only after I exit.

Order my steps so that I do not participate in patterns that weaken, confuse, or destroy.

Teach me how to build.

How to leave cleanly.

How to move without causing harm.

Where something wrong or inappropriate has already been set in motion, give me the Wisdom to interrupt it.

Where stuck patterns or evil cycles persist, help me see them and break them, in the Name of Jesus.

I choose alignment, with You, Lord.

In Jesus' Name, Amen.

IN HIS OWN EYES

Are you the one it happened to… or the one it's happening *through*? Let's locate the truth so it can be corrected.

All the ways of a man are clean in his own eyes. (Proverbs 16:2)

In relationships, family, connections or even in business:

- Do you come to steal, kill, or destroy?
- Did someone do one of those three things to you?
- Are you victim? Or are you the perpetrator?

And Scripture answers, *You may not be able to tell—because you look clean to yourself.* That is what the book has been about.

A man does not begin by identifying himself as harmful. He begins by justifying himself. What he does, he calls necessary. What he takes, he calls deserved. What he damages, he calls unavoidable. In his own eyes… it is clean.

The question is not how it appears to you, Dear Reader. The question is: **What has your presence produced?**

- **Steal** → may feel like "need"
- **Kill** → may feel like "correction"
- **Destroy** → may feel like "justified action"

Self-perception cannot be trusted as the standard because it is hard for one's own eyes to see a man as wrong, imperfect, or sinful. That is why we need the Holy Spirit. He brings conviction because without it, we do not even know if we are breaking the law.

I would not have known sin except through the law. For I would not have known covetousness unless the law had said, 'You shall not covet.
(Romans 7:7)

It was already there… it just hadn't been named.

There are things operating in you that you do not call what they are, until something defines them.

I was alive once without the law, but when the commandment came, sin revived and I died. (Romans 7:9)

He *thought* he was fine, then awareness came. Then everything changed. You can be operating in something… without recognizing it—

until it is revealed. The Old Testament is full of social laws many telling people how to get along with one another. That doesn't stop throughout Scripture.

A new commandment I give unto you, That ye love one another; as I have loved you, that ye also love one another. (John 13:34)

If a man say, I love God, and hateth his brother, he is a liar: for he that loveth not his brother whom he hath
seen, how can he love God whom he hath not seen? (John 14:20)

How are we leaving people that we leave? Should we even be leaving some of those we leave?

Not everyone who steals believes they are a thief. Not everyone who damages believes they are destructive. Not everyone who opens a door believes they caused the breach. Again, because all the ways of a man are clean in his own eyes.

So, the question is not: *Do you think you are right?* The question is: **What does your life say?**

You two met; the structure was intact. Nothing appeared overturned. Nothing visibly missing. And yet… the door was open. It was not forced or broken, but simply open. This meant one of two things: Either something had found a way in… Or something had been allowed.

Something was taken. Or was it given in barter, trade or exchange for something else? Something was weakened. Where it should have been strengthened because two is better than one, it was weakened. Something was brought to ruin.

The danger is not only what was done… The danger is when one, both, or all involved cannot recognize their own place in it.

It is easy to trace what has been done to you. It is harder to consider what has moved through you, because all the ways of a man are clean in his own eyes.

What we call injury, we do not always recognize as something we have also carried. There are patterns that do not begin where we think they do. There are losses that do not originate in a single moment. There are breaches that do not open from one side alone.

What is done… has a way of returning. Not randomly, just when least expected, based on alignment with what has been set in motion. What has been set in motion has been invited, allowed, agreed with, and or propagated by us.

Whatsoever a man soweth, that shall he also reap. (Galatians 6:7)

With the same measure you give, it shall be given back to you. (Luke 6:38)

They have sown the wind and they shall reap the whirlwind. (Hosea 8:7)

Therefore, the question is not only: *Who opened the door?* The question becomes:

What has your life allowed, permitted, or participated in, that made the opening possible?

This is not a judgment or a sentence. This is an opportunity to correct what has been set in motion. Even what is established can be undone if you take the right measures. What has been opened can be closed. What has been set in motion can be brought under authority. there is a pattern… and you may be inside it. In order to get out of it, you have to break the pattern.

The door did not open without a reason, and it didn't open by itself. The structure was intact. Nothing appeared broken. Nothing looked out of place. And yet… something was wrong. The place was always as it had been. The doors were not supposed to be open. Ray and Claudia opened doors they weren't supposed to have opened. Unable to handle what those open doors resulted in the stealing, the killing, and the destroying all the while each of them would tell you that they were only, *dating*.

They didn't use violence, so they thought. They didn't use force, they were just having a nice time and enjoying one another--, opening doors. Open just enough to matter. Which meant something had happened.

When exposed, when wrong doors are open one of our first thoughts may be that nobody told us that we'd need help – so much help to close those doors again. No one told us that we'd need help restoring what was lost, stolen, killed, or destroyed, provided that Mercy is still operational and restoration is still possible.

Those doors were open. Something had been accessed. Something had been allowed. Or something had been taken. At this point, there are only a few questions that matter.

What was done? Who did it? And where were you when it happened?

When something goes sideways— you cannot immediately claim the position of victim, without first examining whether you also participated in what went wrong.

NOW YOU SEE IT

You did not see it at the beginning. You could not have. You could not see it clearly or comprehensively. At the beginning, everything felt different. Connection does that. It draws you in. It narrows your focus. It highlights what is present—and softens what is not yet revealed.

So, you moved. You engaged. You responded. Without fully seeing what was already in motion. But now—you can see it. Not all at once. Not in a single moment. But in pieces that have come together. A pattern that once felt like separate events… now forms a sequence.

What was taken. What was weakened. What was brought to an end. And more importantly—how it happened. Not just through what was done to you, but through what moved through you. That is what has changed, your ability to see it.

Once you can see it—you are no longer moving blindly. You are no longer responding without awareness. You are no longer following something without knowing where it leads. You may not have recognized the pattern at entry, at the beginning, but you recognize it now.

Awareness does something powerful. It interrupts. It slows what once moved automatically. It introduces space—between what is felt… and what is done. In that space, you can choose to build. You can choose to leave without reducing. You can choose not to participate in what you now understand. You cannot control every connection. You cannot prevent every misalignment. But you can govern how you move within it. You can decide what you carry. You can decide what you release. You can decide what you will no longer allow to move through you.

That is where this ends. It ends with a decision about what will happen next. Because now—you can see it. And what you can see—you can change.

Dear Reader:

Thank you for acquiring and reading this book. In Jesus' Name, Amen.

Dr. Marlene Miles

I seal this book, all words, decrees, declarations and prayers herein across every realm, age, era, dimension, and timeline, past present and future and to infinity. I seal them with the Blood of Jesus and the Holy Spirit of Promise.

Let every retaliation against this word, these prayers, these decrees and declarations spoken, prayed, or said by the speaker, or heard by the listener, or anyone praying these words backfire without Mercy, to infinity against the evil perpetrator, in the Name of Jesus. **Amen.**

Christ of God (*The*) 3-book series

Christ of God, (*The*) Box Set, *includes all 3*

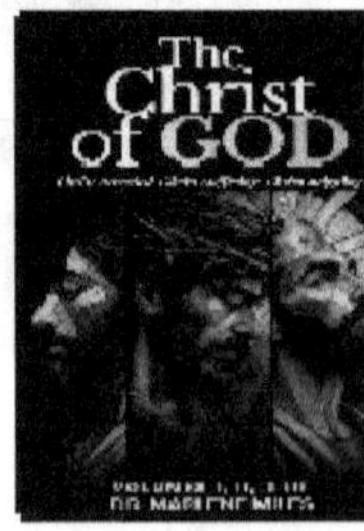

Other books on Authority: **AUTHORITY**

THE INTANGIBLES

HOW A MAN IS OWNED

UNGOVERNED HUNGER

TRIBE

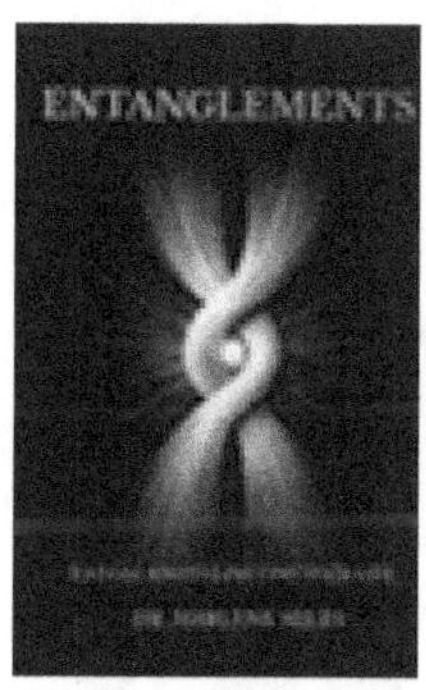

ENTANGLEMENTS: *Illegal Knots Limiting Your Life*

INTO FREEDOM: *Reclaiming Your Authority*

Other Relationship Books by Dr. Marlene Miles:

Already Married in the Spirit: ***Why You May Not Be Married in the Natural*** https://a.co/d/gVSzfQ2

Anti-Marriage, ***The Spirit of*** https://a.co/d/fEKrHFu

The **100 Green Flags Book: Date This Not That and the companion Workbook, DATE THIS NOT THAT WORKBOOK**

Red Flags: The Track Is Not Safe (book & workbook)

Too Many Wives: *Why You Have Lady Problems*

Unbreak My Heart: *Don't Let Me Die*

Why Do I Keep Meeting the Same Guy?

https://a.co/d/0BcAWmW

SOUL TIE book. Soul Tie Workbook. Soul Tie Prayer Manual

Players Gonna Play

Second Marriage, Third--, *Any Marriage*

https://a.co/d/6m6GN4N

Seducing Spirits: Idolatry & Whoredoms

https://a.co/d/4Jq4WEs

Six Men Short: What Has Happened to all the Men?

We Get Along, Right? Compatibility for Couples – (book & workbook)

Matters of the Heart

Made Perfect in Love
https://a.co/d/70MQW3O

Love Breaks Your Heart
https://a.co/d/4KvuQLZ

Unbreak My Heart
https://a.co/d/84ceZ6M

Broken Spirits & Dry Bones
https://a.co/d/e6iedNP

Prayerbooks by this author

While most books by this author have prayer points either throughout the book or at the end, there are some books that are only prayers. You just open up the book and pray.

Prayers Against Barrenness: *For Success in Business and Life*

Fruit of the Womb: *Prayers Against Barrenness*

Beauty Curses, *Warfare Prayers Against*
https://a.co/d/5Xlc2OM

Courts of Marriage: Prayers for Marriage in the Courts of Heaven *(prayerbook)*
https://a.co/d/cNAdgAq

Courtroom Warfare @ Midnight
(prayerbook) https://a.co/d/5fc7Qdp

www.ingramcontent.com/pod-product-compliance
Lightning Source LLC
LaVergne TN
LVHW010951110826
845149LV00015B/3300

* 9 7 8 1 9 7 1 9 3 3 5 0 4 *